MICHAEL DONAGHY

Conjure

PICADOR

First published 2000 by Picador
an imprint of Macmillan Publishers Ltd
25 Eccleston Place, London SW1W 9NF
Basingstoke and Oxford
Associated companies throughout the world
www.macmillan.com

ISBN 0 330 39110 0

1 3 5 7 9 8 6 4 2

A CIP catalogue record for this book is available from
the British Library.

Typeset by SetSystems Ltd, Saffron Walden, Essex
Printed and bound in Great Britain by
Mackays of Chatham plc, Chatham, Kent

for Ruairī Tomās,

HORATIO: It beckons you to go away with it
As if it some impartment did desire
To you alone

Only me, old son.

Acknowledgements

Thanks to the editors of the following magazines, in which some of these poems appeared: *Epoch*, the *Guardian*, the *Independent*, *Metre*, the *New Yorker*, the *New York Times*, the *Observer*, *Poetry (Chicago)*, *Poetry Review*, the *Sunday Times*, the *TLS*, *Verse*.

And many thanks to The Arts Council of England, the Harold Hyam Wingate Foundation, and the Ingram Merrill Foundation (US).

Contents

Conjure

The Excuse

Please hang up. I try again.
'My father's sudden death has shocked us all'
Even me, and I've just made it up,
Like the puncture, the cheque in the post,
Or my realistic cough. As I'm believed,
I'm off the hook. But something snags and holds.

My people were magicians. Home from school,
I followed a wire beneath the table to
A doorbell. I rang it. My father looked up.

Son, when your uncle gets me on the phone
He won't let go. I had to rig up something.

Midnight. I pick up and there's no one there,
No one, invoked, beyond that drone. But if
I had to rig up something, and I do,
Let my excuse be this, and this is true:
I fear for him and grieve him more than any,
This most deceiving and deceived of men . . .
Please hang up and try again.

Not Knowing the Words

Before he wearied of the task, he sang a nightly Mass
for the repose of the souls of the faithful departed
and magicked his blood to bourbon and tears
over the ring, the lock of hair, the dry pink dentures.
Was he talking to her? I never learned.
Walk in, he'd pretend to be humming softly,
like wind through a window frame.

The last I saw of him alive, he pressed me to his coat.
It stinks in a sack in my attic like a drowned Alsatian.
It's his silence. Am I talking to him now, as I get it out
and pull its damp night down about my shoulders?
Shall I take up the task, and fill its tweedy skin?
Do I stand here not knowing the words
when someone walks in?

Caliban's Books

Hair oil, boiled sweets, chalk dust, squid's ink . . .
Bear with me. I'm trying to conjure my father,
age fourteen, as Caliban – picked by Mr Quinn
for the role he was born to play because
'I was the handsomest boy at school'
he'll say, straight-faced, at fifty.
This isn't easy. I've only half the spell,
and I won't be born for twenty years.
I'm trying for rainlight on Belfast Lough
and listening for a small, blunt accent
barking over the hiss of a stove getting louder like surf.
But how can I read when the schoolroom's gone
black as the hold of a ship? Start again.

Hair oil, boiled sweets . . .
But his paperbacks are crumbling in my hands,
seachanged bouquets, each brown page
scribbled on, underlined, memorized,
forgotten like used pornography:
The Pocket Treasury of English Verse,
How to Win Friends and Influence People,
Thirty Days To a More Powerful Vocabulary.

Fish stink, pitch stink, seaspray, cedarwood . . .
I seem to have brought us to the port of Naples,
midnight, to a shadow below deck
dreaming of a distant island.
So many years, so many ports ago!
The moment comes. It slips from the hold
and knucklewalks across the dark piazza
sobbing *maestro! maestro!* But the duke's long dead
and all his magic books are drowned.

Black Ice and Rain

Psalms 6.6

Can I come in? I saw you slip away.
Hors d'oeuvres depress you, don't they? They do me.
And cocktails, jokes . . . such dutiful abandon.
Where the faithful observe immovable feasts
– boat races, birthdays, marriages, martyrdoms –
we're summoned to our lonely ceremonies any time:
B minor, the mouldiness of an old encyclopedia,
the tinny sun snapping off the playground swings,
these are, though we can't know this, scheduled
to arrive that minute of the hour, hour of the day,
day of every year. Again, regular as brickwork,
comes the time the nurse jots on your chart
before she pulls the sheet across your face. Just so,
the past falls open anywhere – even sitting here with you.

Sorry. You remind me of a girl I knew.
I met her at a party much like this, but younger, louder,
the bass so fat, the night so sticky you could drown.
We shouted art at each other over soul
and cold beer in the crowded kitchen and I, at least,
was halfway to a kiss when she slipped
her arm around her friend.
I worked at liking him, and it took work,
and it never got any easier being harmless,
but we danced that night like a three-way game of chess
and sang to Curtis Mayfield pumped so loud
that when I drove them home they could hardly
whisper to invite me up.

Their black walls smirked with Jesus on black velvet
– Jesus, Elvis, Mexican skeletons, big-eyed Virgins,
Rodin's hands clasped in chocolate prayer –
an attitude of decor, not like this room of yours.
A bottle opened – tequila with a cringe of worm –
and she watched me.
Lighting a meltdown of Paschal candles,
she watched me. He poured the drinks rasping
We're seriously into cultural detritus. At which, at last,
she smiled. Ice cubes cracked. The worm sank in my glass.
And all that long year we were joined at the hip.

I never heard them laugh. They had,
instead, this tic of scratching quotes in air –
like frightened mimes inside their box of style,
that first class carriage from whose bright window
I watched the suburbs of my life recede.
          Exactly one year on she let me kiss her – once –
her mouth wine-chilled, my tongue a clumsy guest,
and after that the invitations dwindled.
By Christmas we were strangers. It was chance
I heard about the crash. He died at once.
Black ice and rain, they said. No news of her.

I can't remember why I didn't write.
Perhaps I thought she'd sold the flat and left.

Some nights midway to sleep I'm six years old.
Downstairs it's New Year's Eve. Drink and shrieks.
But my mother's lit the luminous plastic Jesus
to watch me through the night, which is why
I've got my pillow wrapped around my head.
I never hear the door. And when she speaks,
her thick-tongued anger rearing like a beast,
I feel my hot piss spreading through the sheets.
But when I wake, grown up, it's only sweat.
But if I dream, I bleed. A briar crown,
a fist prised open wide, a steadied nail,
a hammer swinging down – the past falls open
anywhere . . .
                    Ash Wednesday evening.
Driving by, I saw her lights were on.
I noticed both their names still on the buzzer
and when I rang I heard her voice. *Come in* –

        her nose was broken, her front teeth gone,
a rosary was twisted round her fists –

        – Come in. I've been saying a novena.
Inside, each crucifix and candle shone
transfigured in her chrysalis of grief.
She spoke about the crash, how she'd been driving,
how they had to cut her from the wreck . . .
and then she slipped and called me by his name.

Of those next hours I remember most
the silences between her sobs, the rain
against the skylight slowly weakening
to silence, silence brimming into sleep and dawn.
Then, having lain at last all night beside her,
having searched at last that black-walled room,
the last unopened chamber of my heart,
and found there neither pity nor desire
but an assortment of religious kitsch,
I inched my arm from under her and left.

    Since then, the calmest voice contains her cry
just within the range of human hearing
and where I've hoped to hear my name gasped out
from cradle, love bed, death bed, there instead
I catch her voice, her broken lisp, his name.
Since then, each night contains all others,
nested mirror-within-mirror, stretching back from then
to here and now, this party, this room, this bed,
where, in another life, we might have kissed.
Thank you, friend, for showing me your things –
you have exquisite taste – but let's rejoin your guests
who must by now be wondering where you've gone.

Our Life Stories

What did they call that ball in *Citizen Kane*?
That crystal blizzardball forecasting his past?
Surely I know the name. Your mum's souvenir
of Blackpool, underwater, in winter –
say we dropped it. What would we say we broke?
And see what it says when you turn it over . . .

I dreamt the little Christmas dome I owned
slipped my soapy fingers and exploded.
Baby Jesus and the Virgin Mother
twitching on the lino like dying guppies.
Let's shake this up and change the weather.

Catch! This marvellous drop, like its own tear,
has leaked for years. The tiny Ferris wheel has surfaced
in an oval bubble where it never snows
and little by little all is forgotten. Shhh!
Let's hold the sad toy storms in which we're held,
let's hold them gingerly above the bed,
bubbles gulping contentedly, as we rock them to sleep,
flurries aswim by our gentle skill,
their names on the tips of our tongues.

Duffel coat. Tennents Extra. No dog.

The rage has eaten the soft of his face away.
He starts to scream before his mouth can open,

screams as Jesus bellowed through the temple
dashing the tables of the dove-vendors and moneychangers,

as Achilles stood on the dyke and loosed the shout that kills,
felling twelve Trojans among their spears and chariots.

Window-rattling, spit-flecked, it peaks, cracks, subsides –
the cry from the tall grass at twilight

from the slow one, the straggler, run out by the herd,
outrun by the lioness.

The Tragedies

Upstage, spotlit, the prince soliloquizes
while courtiers ham their business in the dark.
We see you taking snuff, dim improvisers.
We won't remember, but you've left your mark
within the compass of our sense of sight.

It's how we speed down narrow streets and park.
It's how owls reconnoitre fields by night.

And dimmer, in the wings, the age grows vague
and greyly out of focus. Children die,
a page reports, in papal war and plague.
We glimpse them out the corner of our eye
and see them without looking, without pain.
We aim our minds like arrows at the Dane.

He dies. *Go bid the soldiers shoot.* Applause
like big wings flapping from an autumn field.
Now, as we glance about, the dark withdraws.
The stage dissolves. The orchestra's revealed
as though the light were rising on a tide
past stalls and circle to the streets outside,
as though the vision centred everywhere.

No animal eye can long survive that glare.

> *And let me speak to the yet unknowing world*
> *How these things came about.*
> You caught its eye.
Its talons stretched. A silent wing unfurled.
A shadow glided gently from the sky.

My Flu

I'd swear blind it's June, 1962.
Oswald's back from Minsk. U2s glide over Cuba.
My cousin's in Saigon. My father's in bed
with my mother. I'm eight and in bed with my flu.
I'd *swear*, but I can't be recalling this sharp reek of Vicks,
the bedroom's fevered wallpaper, the neighbour's TV,
the rain, the tyres' hiss through rain, the rain smell.
This would never stand up in court – I'm asleep.

I'm curled up, shivering, fighting to wake,
but I can't turn my face from the pit in the woods
– snow filling the broken suitcases, a boy curled up,
like me, as if asleep, except he has no eyes.
One of my father's stories from the war
has got behind my face and filmed itself:
the village written off the map, its only witnesses
marched to the trees. Now all the birds fly up at once.

And who filmed *this* for us, a boy asleep in 1962,
his long-forgotten room, his flu, this endless rain,
the skewed fan rattling, the shouts next door?
My fever reaches 104. But suddenly he's here,
I'd swear, all round me, his hand beneath my head
until one world rings truer than the other.

The Palm

la connaissance aux cent passages
– René Char

That motorcycle downstairs never starts
but, like a statue with a stomach flu,
disturbs him with its monumental farts.
His phone won't stop. His arts review is due
and must be in the post by half-past three
to make this issue of *Je Suis Partout*.
And here's another *merde* to fuel his rage:
he has to wrestle with a rusty key.
Though they assured him this machine was new,
he's got to press the 'j' against the page
whenever he types *jazz* or *Juiverie*
and he uses these words frequently.
It jams again, the phone rings. Bang on cue,
the motorcycle starts. The curtains part
on the Palm Casino, 1942.

Although he thinks she's buying out the town
the critic's wife sits on an unmade bed
in room 6, naked, as her palm is read
by a guitarist in a dressing gown.
He reels off lines in the forgotten script
that maps her palm: *Here is your first affair . . .*
He looks at her but she can't help but stare
down at the hand in which her hand is gripped.

Rethinking his title, 'For the Masses',
typewriter underarm, the critic passes
in the hallway a trolley of caramelized pears
and a fat man with a string bass case who stares
suspiciously back behind dark glasses.
Could this be M. Vola, room 9, who plays
that nigger music for Vichy gourmets,
hunting the gypsy guitarist in his band?
The critic squints to memorize his face
as the lift cage rattles open for Vola and his bass.
Voilà! He'll call it 'Rhetoric and Race'.

> But back to those pears. Glazed, tanned,
> they fall in behind a whole roast pig
> delivered to the gypsy's room before the gig.
> He watches the waiter watch his crippled hand
> as, with the other, he tries to sign his name.
> He's new at this. It never looks the same.

The typewriter? Dismantled. All the keys
arranged across a workbench side by side.
And the critic hissing *Can I have your name please?*
and *What do you mean you're not qualified?*
and *Shall we call the police judiciaire?*
Tomorrow he will not be everywhere.

> Tonight the gypsy counts in the Quintet.
> They'll play until the curfew lifts at dawn.
> They have to call this foxtrot 'La Soubrette'
> but it's 'I've Got My Love To Keep Me Warm'.

Resolution

The new year blurs the windowpane.
Soho surrenders to the rain
as clouds break over Chinatown.
See how the storm's resolve winds down?
Its steel pins thin and mist away.
Get up. Come here and see the day.

Through this droplet's contact lens,
the West End and the future tense
look dainty, vacant, and convex.
We haven't seen such weather since
the morning they invented sex.
And yet, baptized, by rain and gin,
of last year's unoriginal sins
of inattention and cliché,
this looks like every other day
that we will never see again.

Courage. Coffee. Aspirins.
Our window on the world begins
to dry, the breakfast bulletins
appal, the civil voices lie,
our private garden cloud with doubt.
So let me make *this* crystal clear:
the rain has stopped. Your taxi's here.
The New Year bells will ring you out.

Refusals

Shooting their horses and setting their houses alight,
The faithful struck out for a hillside in Sussex
To wait for the prophesied rapture to take them
At midnight, New Year's Eve, 1899.

But they knelt in the slow, drifting snow singing hymns,
Hushing their children and watching the stars,
Until the sky brightened and the cold sun rose white
Over the plain where their houses still smouldered.

Some froze there all day, some straggled back sobbing
To salvage what little remained of their lives.
Others went mad and refused, till the end of their days,
To believe that the world was still there.

Here, ten seconds to midnight, they join in the count
Over tin horns squealing in the bright drunk rooms.

5:00/5:10/5:15

We shared a dream beneath
a dream-beneath-a-dream.
Our tears became a storm
that washed away our names
and our voices blended with the rain's.
Whatever does the singing sang
about, and then away, the pain
of having been
one creature torn in two.

Then whatever does the waking
woke, or dreamt it woke, to share
our dream-beneath-a-dream
before the primed alarm could tear
us back to me and you.

This is no dream: It's 5:15.
I wake. I pack. Before I go
I'll press my ear against your back –
a hostage at a wall – to hear
one beat. No. Two beats fall.

The Break

Like freak Texan sisters joined at the hip
playing saxophone duets in vaudeville,
we slept leaning, back to back.
When, more and more, our silences deepened,
a new perfume, a phone bill in her padlocked journal,
were props on a stage inside my head
where I woke sweat-drenched, alone.
Now she's gone, I seem to crowd myself because
it takes a second soul to hear the soul,
a third to hear the second . . . they keep coming:
angels many-armed, heraldic chimeras,
two-headed monsters at the map's edge screaming.

Inseparable sisters, I watch you every night
from my half-world, my single mattress.
You are smoking out back between shows
wearing the teal silk double cocktail dress.
You never speak. You pass the smoke,
and the silence between you is a lake on the moon.
Daisy, Violet, you are a girl at a dance
resting for a moment, against a mirror.

Celibates

They're closing down the travelling fair this week.
The crystal balls are packed, the last sword swallowed,
and the geek has shaved and caught the night bus home.
Beyond the dimming generator lights we stick it out,
blind masters of the dying arts, by night, by winter rain,
squatting in the rotting straw of our cages.
The recordreader strokes a disc and snaps back
Gould, *The French Suites*. The booksniffer naps,
face pressed to the uncut pages of the life of Keats
that he has just inhaled. The last haruspicator
snacks on hay with the phrenologist whilst I perform
another brilliant twist in the Mercan Variation
of the Queen's Gambit! History, made, fades away
unseen – as interest in exhibition solo chess
has markedly declined. But you, you inspire us,
frighten us, with your extraordinary abstinence,
obscurity and silence. Only a soft chittering
tells me you're there now, naked, knitting,
with tweezers, small flames – dark gold flash
of brass foil, spring coil, and gear – into tonight's
unsold array of clockwork crickets.

Reprimands

John 20:24–29

We fell out of love as toddlers fall
glancing down, distracted, at their feet,
as the pianist in the concert hall
betrays her hands to thought and adds an extra
beat –
The thought vertiginous. The reprimand.
It fells the bee mid-flight. It made me stall
before a holy water font in Rome
half afraid that if I dipped my hand
I'd find the water's surface hard as stone
and – this you'd never understand –
half afraid to leave the thing alone.
For I'd been taught that Jesus walked the sea
and came to Peter three leagues out of port.
Said Peter *Bid me to come unto thee*
and strode on faith dryfoot until he thought . . .
and thinking, sank. I'd never learnt to swim
but I'd seen insects skim across a pond
and I'd seen glasses filled above the brim.
Some firm conviction keeps a raindrop round.
What kept me rigid as a mannequin?

We fell out of love and nearly drowned.
The very wordlessness all lovers want
to feel beneath their feet like solid ground
dissolved to silences no human shout
could ripple –
                        like the surface of that font
when other voices, tourist and devout,

grew still, and someone whispered by my side
O ye of little faith – and shallow doubt –
choose here to wet that hand or stand aside.
No one was there. But I could tell that tone.
I heard his ancient apostolic voice
this evening when I went to lift the phone
to tell you this – and froze. The reprimand.
For once, in two minds, Thomas made the choice
to bless and wet with blood his faithless hand.

The Drop

We taped it under the seats,
packed it into the door panels,
drove it over the mountains in July,
and the other two hadn't a word of the language
not a word, not *help*, not *food*,
and always that fear of the sirens and lights, until,
at the end, we drove all night screaming
our throats raw over the radio to keep awake,
words we didn't understand, *mi corazón*,
every other word, *mi corazón*, then,
an hour to dawn the day of the drop, we drove down
through Calvária – just hours to go, but
we turned off the road near a fairground to dodgems,
carousel, all boarded up, spent fires, an old starving bitch
limping loose through the trailers. To nothing.

We got out to piss then waited for dawn in the car.
After days on the road we were talked out, hoarse,
but this was different, I remember, I *think* I remember,
paint peeling on the hoardings, the sun floating up
red through the dust and mesquite smoke. Crows.
The place seemed emptied even of ourselves.
And then we drove on to the drop.

I'd forgotten, and you never asked . . .
But it all came back last night. Trouble outside –
a speeding siren woke me, tuning down a fifth,
and I realized I'd been dreaming of that morning,
the three of us sitting in the car and, somehow,
I was standing outside too, watching us. I couldn't speak
because I'd used up all the words.

But it was the words had used me up
and left me black birds, a white dog, and *corazón*.
But this was years ago. Years. Before I met you.
The money? It went where money goes.

Where is it written that I must end here,

incipit, a great gold foliate Q surrounding my garden wherein nuns fiddle, philosophers discourse on the augmented fourth, the $\sqrt{-1}$? A window opens, a wax cylinder crackles, and the castrato's trill is borne on the wind to the skating peasantry. Across the frozen lake two boys set fire to a cat; here, the first of thirteen bears in the Queen's bear garden, its eyes scooped out, its nose blown full of pepper, shakes two mastiffs from its back and bellows; the youngest barn burner to be hanged is eight. His parents are made to watch. Here, beyond the scaffold and the smoke, a distant hill. On the hill a windmill; in its engine room a desk; on the desk a psalter; scrawled in its margin a prayer in the shape of a conch; in that prayer a devil-snare wound in a spiral of words. I would be the demon seduced by the riddle, lost in the middle, who cannot read back.

from The Deadly Virtues

iv. Faith

Three hundred gathered at the Angel of the North.
The crowds looked up at Blackpool Pier.
The crowds looked up so they could tell their children's children
They'd witnessed the occlusion of his iris.
At noon, at more than a thousand miles an hour,
his shadow raced across the Channel and silenced the birds.
For a moment the predator's vertical pupil dilated
as his children raised their faces and returned, through tears,
through treated glass, through welders' masks,
the gaze they had avoided all their lives.

vii. Justice

She's invisible because she's blind.
She can't be ugly. She has no face.
She will check that each confession's signed
and weigh each individual case.
She has no tongue but the final word.
She has no body. She is everyone.
It is she who bears the scales, the sword,
and noose and cattle prod and gun.

Timing

Yes I know it's not funny. A prisoner told me
when I was an orderly during the war,
exactly the way that I told it, the whores and the mice.
I say told though I should say he gargled or grunted –
we'd built him a jaw out of one of his ribs
so it took him some time. When he got near the end
and my tunic was freckled with mucus and blood
and the mask of my face ached from grinning
he pulled me down close for the punch line.
He said it. I waited – the way that you waited just now –
but its door never opened.

                      I'm sure that was it,
word for word, though he had neither English nor lips,
because after I searched what remained of his face
he started the torture again. An infection, I reckoned,
and dabbed at his wound and returned to my rounds
but it buzzed round my head like a wasp. Was it code?
If he took me for one of his own in his fever
what might he betray? I ran back at first light
but he'd died in the night of pneumonia.

I'm sure there are those men who laugh out of etiquette,
bafflement, fear of appearing obtuse, or just fear,
and men who dismiss it, or lose it, or change it
before it begins to change them.
Only one in a thousand, perhaps, will remember,
exactly, repeat it, exactly the way that I tell it.
I knew when you hailed me tonight at the station,
I said to myself, as you climbed in the back, he's the one.

Irena of Alexandria

Creator, thank You for humbling me.
Creator, who twice empowered me to change
a jackal to a saucer of milk,
a cloud of gnats into a chandelier,
and once, before the emperor's astrologers,
a nice distinction into an accordion,
and back again, thank You
for choosing Irena to eclipse me.

She changed a loaf of bread into a loaf of bread,
caused a river to flow downstream,
left the leper to limp home grinning and leprous,
because, the bishops say, Your will burns
bright about her as a flame about a wick.

Thank You, Creator, for taking the crowds away.
Not even the blind come here now.
I have one bowl, a stream too cold to squat in,
and the patience of a saint. Peace be,
in the meantime, upon her. And youth.
May sparrows continue to litter her shoulders,
children carpet her footsteps in lavender,
and may her martyrdom be beautiful and slow.

A Nun's Story

i.m. N.C.

That's Timmy, with his eyes shut
in our class photo snapped by Diane Arbus
before her *Vogue* days. If he grew up,
he swore, he'd devote his life to God.
Sister Tim. He stole *A Nun's Story*
and acted out scenes from *Black Narcissus*
wearing the hood of his sweatshirt up,
habitually. We studied together
in his kitchen when we were ten.
Above the table hung icons of the Kennedys,
DeValera, and Tim's black-belt dad
splitting a plank with his bare foot.
We lost touch at fifteen, as if he'd entered
a silent order. Perhaps he has. But I think
Sister Tim chainsmokes. I think
he lives with a Cuban bodybuilder
in the East Village, having, like everyman
in his season, a true vocation.

Local 32B

(US National Union of Building Service Workers)

The rich are different. Where we have doorknobs,
they have doormen – like me, a cigar store Indian
on the Upper East Side, in polyester, in August.
As the tenants tanned in Tenerife and Monaco
I stood guard beneath Manhattan's leaden light
watching poodle turds bake grey in half an hour.
Another hot one, Mr Rockefeller!
An Irish doorman foresees his death,
waves, and runs to help it with its packages.
Once I got a cab for Pavarotti. No kidding.
No tip either. I stared after him down Fifth
and caught him looking after me, then through me,
like Samson, eyeless, at the Philistine chorus –
Yessir, I put the tenor in the vehicle.
And a mighty tight squeeze it was.

Regarding Our Late Correspondence

Often I'll begin to write to you
and find I'm simply copying the plot,
that glass machine that dictates what we do.
    And often I'll be chalking up a cue,
clocking each ball rolling towards its slot
in that web of vectors
        – and I'm *crap* –

But it's my balance makes me miss my shot;
balancing the angle of my aim
against the random factors of the nap,
    or point of impact, say, or force, or weight,
or the chance of having missed the game
or having turned up pissed,
        an hour late.

But like I said, I'm crap at games.
I know. We know we can't finesse what's been.
we only have that instant of our skill,
    to squint across a field of abstract green,
or print *forgive me* in unbroken script,
sharpening the focus of our will
on making what comes next be
        what we mean . . .

which is where my aim has always slipped,
as often, in the night, I freeze mid-dream.
Just before I wake and lose the drift,
    a soft *clack* startles me, I turn towards you,
a million miniature pistons shift
the spindly camshaft of a vast machine
beneath the rumbling as the last balls drop.
    As, often, I'll begin to write to you,
        and stop.

Tears

are shed, and every day
workers recover
the bloated cadavers
of lovers or lover
who drown in cars this way.

And they crowbar the door
and ordinary stories pour,
furl, crash, and spill downhill –
as water will – not orient,
nor sparkling, but still

The River in Spate

sweeps us both down its cold grey current.
Grey now as your father was when I met you,
I wake even now on that shore where once,
sweat slick and still, we breathed together –
in – soft rain gentling the level of the lake,
out – bright mist rising from the lake at dawn.
How long before we gave each other to sleep,
to air – drawing the mist up, exhaling the rain?
Though we fight now for breath and weaken
in the torrent's surge to the dark of its mouth,
you are still asleep in my arms by its source,
small waves lapping the gravel shore,
and I am still awake and watching you,
in wonder, without sadness, like a child.

The Pallace of Memoria
garnished with Perpetuall Shininge
Glorious Lightes Innumerable

It's shut. And after such a climb!
A caustic drizzle slicks the deserted funicular railway
as the lights come on below in the abandoned weekend.
The distant band's just tuning up in the life you missed.
Your beloved dead are back there
getting dressed for their garden parties.
Yours was among the first families of Purgatory.

When you return now to your ancestral gardens
you hear always an orchestra distantly, carefully,
mimicking the rain, or the sobbing of your national bird.
When you enter the deserted manor
you are often met by the police, who recognize you, bow,
and torture you by weeping during their inquiries
as is the custom of your country.

Annie

Flicker, stranger. Flare and gutter out.
The life you fight for is the light you kept.
That task has passed this hour from wick to window.
Fade you among my dead my never-daughter.

Upriver in your mother's blood and mine
it's always night. Their kitchen windows burn
whom we can neither name nor say we loved.
Go to them and take this letter with you.

Go let them pick you up and dandle you
and sing you lullabies before the hob.

April 28th, 1940

    the clear cold of it that morning this was nine
when the milkman's daughter had been sent round
that morning to show us her first communion dress
and I spilt tea on the linen and the stain
spread this was nine and my mother fussed over her
as the sirens started up the clear cold above
that morning the stain spread in the air sent round
that morning to show us her first communion dress
and bundled her out the door to run the few yards
home and the stain spread in the clear sky she was nine
when we crawled from the cellar that morning we found
our roof blown clean away to the clear cold above
on my bicycle down to see the smoking street and her house
gone to shingles and bricks and timber and armchairs and glass
and her father was sobbing and calling her name
and I looked in their garden to the white dress soaked
red to the waist and the stain spread

Needlework

tattoos commissioned for the
1999 'Last Words' poetry festival, Salisbury

i

Copy this across your heart,
Whisper what your eyes have heard,
To summon me when we're apart,
This word made flesh, this flesh made word.

ii

The serpent sheds her skin and yet
The pattern she'd as soon forget
Recalls itself. By this I swear
I am the sentence that I bare.

proportion

Who fit that sash in the back window? And
who took this snapshot of us at the airport,
tilting your camera woozily? Whose thumb
occludes us? Are we crying before this
stranger? Who saved it, creased it,
smoothed it, fixed it to black paper by four
right-angle triangles? No master framer
reckoning by golden section, no
journeyman riffling soft curls of cedar to
vines, cornets, *putti* and *fleurs de lys*. No.
Whoever fit that bastard sash out back
queered it at such a slant you've got to ram
the heel of your hand slam up against it –
good, white-glossed Protestant pine, plain
as the pane that rattles when it shuts

The Years

Penetrar el espejo, faceless gods,
Cagers of the heart's four crowded rooms,
Guardians of crossroads, breakers of locks,
Openers of tombs,
      Rise up rise up from the floor of this house
Up the veins of my leg like a riptide.
Darklings, listen, I am your last gamble.
I am bridled and saddled. Enter the stable.
I am yours to ride.

      When the windows slammed shut
Through the gang-raped summer
And meths-soaked rags ignited in the dives,
You held us down, defiler of dreams,
You struck the matches, you opened the knives.
      When the rivet shot
Through my father's boot
And he tracked bloody prints on the factory floor,
You threw him the mop, degrader of souls,
You made him clock out, you showed him the door.
      And when I lay awake
To the gargling drain
Or the curtain rippled sun across the wall,
You mopped my forehead, mother of whispers,
You bathed me in sleep, you let the night fall.

      Pick up the phone. I'm alone on the corner.
Fill in my timesheet, I'll help you remember.
Peel my face from the glass, lift my foot from the brake,
Run the film backwards, rewind the tape.
      Penetrar el espejo, bastard powers
Of the brick through the window and the drunken kiss,
How could I put any one god before you?
How would I know any world but this?

Mine

How long is a piece of string?
I give it maybe twenty years. From my beginning
to his end, a cable jerks tight, sings, twists, and frays.
   And if you enter, how will you get back?
But that's where you come in.
I'll be down there reeling out this line
behind me like a diver's air hose. Hold this.
I'll only be gone a moment.
   How long is a moment?
A mile of eighteen-inch seam in anthracite,
six inches of mainspring in an unwound clock,
the time it takes, the time that's taken from it.
And I've already slammed the lift cage shut.
   Are these the sacrificed?
No. They're only sleeping underground
as searchlights cross in the cloud over London
and tunnels honeycomb below in the dark
of my father's dreams. And they are the sacrificed.
   And if I entered how would I . . .
Back outside I fight to catch my breath
and squeeze around, but now I'm sure I'm lost.
The tunnels fork, detour and reconnect
and circles within circles corkscrew back
to one faint star, or luminous dial of a watch
down a well, which, as I near, expands
into a thumbprint, maelstrom, weather system.
Swept up in its spiral arms, I'm dragged
down deeper, to the centre, to the freak
whose den now opens out around me –
– an airless room of baby food and wheelchairs
where the nurse arrives through muslin-filtered light
to hoover, plump, switch off *Columbo*,
and bring to the ancient bull-headed bastard its bedpan.
And when, at last, it lifts its fleshy, palsied,
toothless, half-blind, almost human head,

it's me.
        Whom did you expect? it retches
from its blackened lung, *I'm not your father,*
son. Mine is a worked-out seam whose walls
get disappeared, caved-in, carved out.
Back out of it now, before you lose your thread.
Go home, unpick the knot you've made,
leave it skitter in long waves across the tarmac
unspooled like the guts of a crushed cassette,
pay out whatever bloody yarn you must
though it wind through olive grove, ruin,
renamed road at first light where you're last seen walking,
just, to the rest of your own life, whoever you are,
and no king's daughter holding the end of your line.

A Messenger

With no less purpose than the swifts
that scrawl my name across the sky,
the hand of an obsessed pianist
quivers inches from my face.

She's anchored so she hangs mid-air
like an angel in a Christmas play.
As fidgety, but tinier, and she's forgot
her only line, *Fear not.*

With no less purpose,
than her prey, the fritillary,
flicks a wing and swells the Yangtze,
she's spun a filament across my path.

I could no more cross this line
and wreck her morning's work
than graph the plot that brought me
eye to compound eye with her.

I'd worry for her, out so far
on such tenuous connections,
but the crosshairs of the gunsight
are implied in her precision.

Quease

for P.F. *mea culpa*

Welcome to the afterlife. Or life.
I'd know that clammy pallor anywhere,
the vertigo that Chuang Tzu must have felt
who dreamt he was a butterfly, just once,
then spent a lifetime puking up his rice
because he really *was* a butterfly
now dreaming he was Chuang Tzu. Breathe.
Sailors say to look at the horizon,
the edge from which you've lately plummeted.
Trust me. I'm a connoisseur of quease.

Do you want the vomitorium?
I've fitted out an ancient Orgone Box,
although I rarely get that far myself,
and being closed in only makes it worse.
Too many bouts bareknuckled with amnesia,
I'd wake up in a cubicle in detox,
or clawing at the lining of my coffin,
or in a proper job. That kind of thing.

Quease builds a portaloo about itself,
a lift that takes one passenger, then drops.
You tell the wife you need fresh air or fags
then sprint six blocks to find a working phone
to dial your other life. It isn't home.
Now listen to the message that you leave:
before it trips your gag reflex, look down.
Someone, something, got this far tonight.
You're standing in its pizza of despair.

It all goes back to the Confessional,
the Inquisition's passport photo booth,
just room enough to kneel and stash your gum
as boozy Father Mick slid back the screen,
already wheezing with concern to hear
how many times you'd touched yourself down there.
Who's here to blame you, or forgive you, now,
for all those lies about the lies you told,
the cats you blinded and the rats you boiled?

That's why you're not feeling quite yourself,
and why I'm talking for the two of us:
your jaw's estranged by novocaine. You're stuck
halfway between the face you got from God
– like something drawn in crayon by a child –
and the one you make up as you go,
which is even worse. I know this phiz.

Halfway into jeans that aren't me,
I've caught its profile in the fitting room,
or watched its blankness settle in the pools
of the thousand tiny downstairs loos
where I knelt in Technicolor prayer.
Once it blurred across a room-sized bed
across the ceiling of a bed-sized room.
And once, it spoke. It tapped a camera plate
and whispered in the voice of Father Mick
There's no one here but you and me and God.
Say Cheese. The flash was like an angry slap.

So when you wake tomorrow wrapped in silk
inches from some mask in which you read
the corpse complexion of the urge to purge,
the pig sweat of the will to keep it down,
when you wake and try to wriggle free
into the sunlight of your adult stage,
stop. Listen for the whizz of tiny gears.
Imago that dreams our meeting here,
the sheet you're trapped in may not be your own.

Here comes the warden fiddling with the keys.
Here comes the porter with a mop and pail.
Here comes your priest and executioner,
your co-star, foil, or rude mechanical,
a noisy wind-up spider cut from tin,
Made in China on its abdomen.
You just try telling it *There's no one here.*
Feeling better? Here it comes again.
Absolvum Te, son. Better out than in.

Umbrage

Let them speak now
who have so long lain at our feet.
For far too long, like stricken lovers,
we have watched them sleep.

Or ignored them. Let them rise up,
freakishly tall in the level evening sun.
Let their dark voices ring in our skulls.
Let them speak, at long last, as one.

Haunts

Don't be afraid, old son, it's only me,
though not as I've appeared before,
on the battlements of your signature,
or margin of a book you can't throw out,
or darkened shop front where your face
first shocks itself into a mask of mine,
but here, alive, one Christmas long ago
when you were three, upstairs, asleep,
and haunting *me* because I conjured you
the way that child you were would cry out
waking in the dark, and when you spoke
in no child's voice but out of radio silence,
the hall clock ticking like a radar blip,
a bottle breaking faintly streets away,
you said, as I say now, *Don't be afraid.*

December 27 1999

Some Notes

The Break – Daisy and Violet Hilton were the Siamese Twins in Todd Browning's 1933 film *Freaks*.

Reprimands – In the Gospels, the name of the apostle Thomas is always accompanied by the epithet 'the twin'.

The Years – *Penetrar el espejo*, 'Penetrate the mirror', a Santeria invocation. The spirits are invited to emerge from the mirror's surface and inhabit the body of the supplicant.

The Palm – Django Reinhardt and one 'P. DeMan' stayed at the same hotel in Cannes in 1942, the Palm, where Reinhardt was playing. Louis Vola was the bassist and manager of Reinhardt's band, The Hot Club de France.

Conjure – L. *conjurare*, to swear together, a double oath.